What Christians
Should Know About...

Discerning of Spirits

John Edwards

Sovereign World

Copyright © 2000 John Edwards

ISBN: 1 85240 277 6

Scripture quotations are taken from
The HOLY BIBLE, NEW INTERNATIONAL VERSION.
Copyright © 1973, 1978, 1984 by International Bible Society.
Used by permission.

The publishers aim to produce books which will help to extend and
build up the Kingdom of God. We do not necessarily agree with every view
expressed by the author, or with every interpretation of Scripture expressed.
We expect each reader to make his/her judgement in the light of their own
understanding of God's Word and in an attitude of Christian love and fellowship.

SOVEREIGN WORLD LIMITED
P.O. Box 777, Tonbridge, Kent TN11 0ZS, England

Typeset by CRB Associates, Reepham, Norfolk.
Printed in the UK by Phase Print, Nottingham.

Contents

1

In at the Deep End

Picking up the gauntlet
In 1979 I received a prophecy that changed the course of my
Christian service and the ministry of New Life Christian Centre
Croydon – a ministry that has now seen many thousands of
people set free from the torment of evil spirits.

An evangelistic team who had been holding tent crusades
across the UK, had come to our church to conduct a series of
meetings. The three who worked together at that time were
Andrew Shearman, Clyde Sandry and Robert Ferguson. They
had witnessed manifestations of evil spirits in some of their
crusades, especially when they had prayed for those who came
forward in response to the gospel message, or when they
encouraged those in the tent to enthusiastically praise and
worship the Lord.

During their stay in Croydon we talked together of these
experiences and of how God was moving in each of our lives.
We all had a desire to see the power of God at work, and a
longing for demonstrations of healing and miracles. One
evening we were having a time of prayer together in my home
when Clyde spoke a very strong prophecy over me. He said that
he saw Satan in front of me throwing down a gauntlet and that
if I responded to the challenge the Lord would give me power
over evil spirits and they would tremble before me. Clyde went
on to warn that if I accepted this opportunity it would be a
lonely walk and I would be misunderstood and ostracised by
many, but that the Lord would be with me. In my heart I was
impressed as to the seriousness of the challenge and decided
before the Lord that I would take it up.

A few days later I shared this prophecy with one of the elders of our church. He told me that same week someone had approached him requesting prayer for deliverance, and here was an opportunity to act on the promise I had received.

The man who had asked for help was in his forties and, I later discovered, had been brought up in a Satanist family and had been involved with occult practices for most of his life. I made an appointment to see him one evening the following week, together with the elder and another brother. I had never prayed for deliverance for anyone before that night, but had read what Jesus had done and what some others had experienced. While waiting for this man to arrive I had the strong impression that before we began to cast out spirits I should 'bind him in his chair'. Not literally bind him with a rope, but speak over him in the name of Jesus that he was bound in the chair. This proved to be the leading of the Holy Spirit, because later when demons were manifesting in him and speaking out of him, they claimed that they wanted to attack us but were unable to as the man could not leave his chair.

After talking with the man for a few moments we prayed asking the Lord's help, 'bound him' in his chair, then commanded the evil spirits to leave him. Immediately demons began to speak out of the man. They were angry, boastful and vindictive. For three hours this process continued and a number of spirits left him, but by no means all of them. It was like undergoing a crash course in deliverance and when I drove home in the early hours of the morning my head was reeling with what I had seen and heard that night. I would not recommend that anyone praying for deliverance for the first time take on such an extreme case as this.

I continued to have some contact with this man for a few months, but sadly there was no willingness on his part to make a clean break from his old lifestyle. To live in freedom demands a turning away from all uncleanness and a determination to follow Christ as Lord.

Breaking a curse
A few days after this first experience in deliverance I drove

5

across London to my brother Philip's home to talk to him about what I was discovering, and to tell him that he probably needed to be set free in some areas. I had begun to see that traumatic experiences in people's lives could result in evil spirits entering, and, knowing something of my brother's life, had a conviction that I should see him and encourage him to receive prayer.

The first thing that struck me upon arriving at his home, was the design of the stained glass in his front door – although I'd never noticed it before, it now appeared to me as evil. I went in and spoke to my brother and his wife Daphne about some of the things I had been experiencing, suggesting that Philip may also need some deliverance. As I was standing with them in the hall, the telephone rang. It was the rugby club to which my brother belonged with some details for him about their next game. As I watched my brother talking on the phone I seemed to see in his face that he was in bondage to the game of rugby, it had become the ruling passion of his life. Without thinking I took the phone from him and said to the person on the other end 'Philip will not be playing rugby any more' and put the phone down. My brother was surprised but never uttered a word of complaint!

Later, approaching the front door again as I was about to leave, I told Philip and Daphne that I felt there was something wrong with the pattern of the glass and that I wanted to break it. They told me to do whatever I wanted, so collecting a carving knife from the kitchen, I used the handle to knock out the panes from the leaded window. As I tapped out the glass, one piece didn't fall out like the others, but flashed across my face as if some evil force sought to cut and harm me. At that same moment Daphne, who was standing behind me, gave a cry and put her hand to her heart. As the window was being broken she felt a great weight lift off her chest.

After this incident, with the glass in their front door broken and everything in upheaval, I left them to return to Croydon. That evening another Christian friend joined Philip and his wife and they began to pray as I had suggested and seek the Lord together. Suddenly Philip was thrown out of his chair and on to the floor, as an evil spirit began manifesting. That night he was set free from a number of evil spirits.

I discovered later that the pattern on Philip's door represented two bull's horns piercing a heart. My brother's house is situated on a bend in the road, and there had often been quite serious accidents there. From the day the glass was broken there was a drastic reduction in the number of road accidents outside the house. A curse appeared to have been broken with the removal of the symbol from the door. It also transpired that for some time before my visit, Daphne had been seeing a black shape in the house. From that day onwards this form never appeared again.

It gradually dawned on me that the impression I had about the door, and the sudden awareness of the control my brother was under were examples of 'discerning of spirits'. The authority I had received to contend with demonic powers had brought the gift of discerning of spirits into operation in my life.

Soon after this rather dramatic introduction to deliverance, Philip also became involved in full-time Christian ministry and has since had a strong anointing for praying for others to be set free. In his ministry I can see God's purposes being worked out, and I thank the Lord for constraining me to travel across London to my brother's house that day.

'Lord show me the truth'

What had led up to the prophetic promise that had thrust me so dramatically into this new realm? Although brought up in a Bible-believing church that was open to the gifts of the Holy Spirit, I had never received any teaching about deliverance and had never witnessed anyone receiving deliverance. In my early twenties I heard a taped message played at the end of a young people's meeting that mentioned Christians being set free from evil spirits, but at the time we considered it foolish because it was so strongly opposed by our pastor. We accepted his teaching that a Christian could not have an evil spirit, and so our minds were set. Many church leaders today resolutely refuse to consider that a Christian may need to be set free from indwelling evil spirits. The result of this stubbornness is that believers in their churches and fellowships are cut off from the possibility of hearing teaching about deliverance and receiving the help they often desperately need.

This teaching made it very difficult for me to accept that a believer might need deliverance. I realise now that it is one of Satan's ploys to close the minds of Christians to the possibility; this keeps in bondage those who should be set free and handicaps many in the Church from growing and living joyful, victorious lives.

I became increasingly aware of the need for people to be set free by talking with others who ministered to people in this way, and by reading various books on the subject of deliverance. My wife and I had observed that some people we counselled and prayed with never seemed to change, but remained with their fears, depression, controlling habits and other problems, and so we began to seek the Lord for some answers. I came to the place where I prayed 'Lord, if it is true that some Christians need deliverance, please show me.' That proved to be one of the most important steps on my journey; if our minds are totally closed to something, then God rarely obliges us to see the truth. However, when we seek Him, willing to set aside our preconceived ideas, He will always lead us into the truth. My experience has been that those who are the most vehemently opposed to deliverance are generally in need of being set free themselves – the enemy within setting up the opposition.

Deliverance in the church
Soon after my first experience of praying for deliverance, and the strange experiences at my brother's house, we began to see strange new happenings in our church. It had always been our custom to invite people to come forward and receive prayer during our Sunday services, particularly in the morning meeting. Now as we prayed for people – confirming the prophecy that had stated 'evil spirits will tremble before you' – we observed that some would begin to tremble and shake as we laid hands upon them in the name of Jesus. Demons were manifesting exactly as the prophecy said they would. I was most surprised, not least because at that time I would not have

8

associated the problems we were praying for – people simply feeling sick or unwell – with the need for deliverance. Neither would I have thought those receiving prayer were the sort of people who might be troubled by evil spirits. The Holy Spirit however, was causing the spirits to manifest so that they could be dealt with.

As I continued to pray for deliverance for various brothers and sisters in the church, I began to appreciate the different ways in which the Holy Spirit is able to give the discernment that is necessary for those involved in this work.

Sharing the burden
There were a number of people who received deliverance in public meetings, but the majority received help during times of private counselling and prayer. This has continued to be the case in our fellowship for the past twenty years.

My wife Doris and I continued to pray for those who sought our help – both those who attended our fellowship and a growing number who contacted us from other churches. There was no need to publicise the fact that we were praying for deliverance – the news spread like wildfire! Such were the needs in peoples lives, the phone never seemed to stop ringing. They were mainly Christians who were asking to see us, and often in total desperation. It soon became clear that we were unable to meet the demands being placed upon us and others needed to become involved in this ministry. Over a number of weeks we ran a course on how to minister deliverance, and several others in the church began to be share in the work of releasing the captives – most noticeably those who themselves had been ministered to in this way. As these new recruits became involved they also began to receive revelation and the Holy Spirit's help in discernment when they prayed with those in need. It seems to be that whenever we go forward in the work of the kingdom that the various gifts of the Spirit begin to operate in our lives.

Why this booklet?
My purpose in writing this is to tell the story of some of our experiences since becoming involved in deliverance ministry

and to explain the various ways in which the Holy Spirit can communicate revelation to us when we are confronted by the demonic. It is hoped that as you read this book you will be encouraged, and become able to understand more clearly the battle we are all engaged in. It might even help you to see that the gift of discerning of spirits has already been operating in your life without you realising it.

2

The Unseen World

'O Lord, open his eyes'

The younger man turned with panic towards his master 'Oh my Lord what shall we do?' The two had gone out from the city of Dothan early that morning and had found it surrounded by a strong force of armed men – soldiers from Syria, mounted men and chariots, sent out by order of the King of Aram to capture Elisha the prophet, the young man's master.

Elisha had been advising the King of Israel of the deployment of the King of Aram's forces. God had been revealing supernaturally to His prophet the secret plans of the invaders, who were thus being thwarted in their attacks upon Israel. 'Don't be afraid' Elisha replied to the youth's anxious cry, 'Those who are with us are more than those who are with them.' The prophet then prayed, 'O Lord, open his eyes so that he may see.' Immediately, the servant could see the hills full of horsemen, and chariots of fire around Elisha protecting him from the danger. This angelic army that the youth was shown so dramatically, had been there all the time for the protection of the prophet, but had not been visible with normal sight. God caused the servant to be aware of the spiritual forces present that day, so that he saw the angels in the form of horsemen and charioteers. He discerned supernaturally the spirit beings gathered there.

This intriguing incident of supernatural discernment, recorded in 2 Kings 6:8–23, resulted in the ending of Syria's raids into Israel at that time.

Satan at his elbow

Another example of spiritual powers being revealed was when

the prophet Zechariah was shown the high priest Joshua being accused by Satan. Zechariah was being given an understanding of the spiritual conflict that was taking place following the return of exiled Jews to Jerusalem from Babylon.

Zechariah 3:1 says, *'Then he showed me Joshua the high priest standing before the angel of the LORD, and Satan standing at his right side to accuse him.'* This revelation went on to explain the Lord's gracious provision for the high priest and his rebuke of Satan. The demonically inspired opposition to the rebuilding of the temple would be overcome and Zechariah was to encourage his people to trust in God by sharing this vision with them.

We also need the Lord to give us revelation in order to know precisely what spiritual powers are at work in our lives and in the affairs of our communities and nations.

Walking by faith not by sight
Generally we are not able to see or detect spirits with our natural senses, however the Scriptures make it clear that our lives are often being influenced, and at times coerced, by spiritual beings – both angels and demons.

Even though the spirit world is hidden, we are challenged to live our lives as Christians not according to that which we receive through our senses, but according to that which is revealed to us by God's Word. That is, we are to 'walk by faith not by sight.' So it is when reading the Psalms we are encouraged by the statement that *'the angel of the LORD encamps around those who fear him, and he delivers them'* (Psalm 34:7). We do not necessarily 'see' the angel of the Lord, but know that he is there.

The Apostle Paul's words of exhortation to the believers at Ephesus tell us that, *'... our struggle is not against flesh and blood, but against the rulers, against the authorities, against the powers of this dark world and against the spiritual forces of evil in the heavenly realms'* (Ephesians 6:12). Accepting this we are better able to understand the spiritual implications of everyday circumstances. It explains why some people act against the people of God as they do.

12

When we live out our lives as Christians, being guided by God's Word rather than what we see around us, God is pleased and our faith is strengthened. However there are times when we need additional insight, either for our protection, or to make us more effective in our Christian walk. Then it is necessary for God to 'lift the veil', so that we might know clearly those things usually hidden from us.

God's provision for us

God desires that the Church be equipped for moving in the realm of the supernatural and exercising the authority delegated to her by the risen Christ, who has power over all things. Jesus rose from the dead, and the Father *exalted him to the highest place and gave him the name that is above every name, that at the name of Jesus every knee should bow . . . '* (Philippians 2:9–10). It was with an emphasis on that authority, and with the assurance of His always being with them, that Jesus sent His disciples into all nations to make disciples (Matthew 28:18). His being with them was achieved by the indwelling of the Holy Spirit who came as the promised Comforter. Immediately before returning to His Father, Jesus had promised His disciples that they would receive power when the Holy Spirit came upon them.

The history of the early Church, set out in the Acts of the Apostles, shows this power being demonstrated in healings and miracles, and also in the revelation and understanding that was granted to believers in the early Church by the Holy Spirit. Knowing their spiritual enemies made them more effective in their warfare – they were able to fight with precision and not just 'beat the air'.

During this last century there has seen a rediscovery of the New Testament understanding of the person of the Holy Spirit and a renewed experience of His power. Firstly in the Pentecostal Movement at the beginning of the century, then later with the charismatic renewal and the outpourings of the Holy Spirit that have followed.

Today the use of the gifts of the Holy Spirit is recognised all over the world. Speaking in tongues, prophecies, and healing in the name of Jesus are widely accepted, and the principles of spiritual warfare and deliverance from the power of evil spirits, are being taught wherever God the Holy Spirit is at work.

Effective witnesses

On the day of Pentecost ten days after Jesus ascended into heaven, the disciples began to fulfil the command of Jesus by becoming 'witnesses' to Him. Their proclamation of Jesus, alive from the dead, was carried out in the power of the Holy Spirit and signs and wonders accompanied their preaching. The book of Acts is an exciting record of 'God working with them'.

> *'Everyone was filled with awe, and many wonders and miraculous signs were done by the apostles.'*   (Acts 2:43)

One of the ways the Holy Spirit moved through the apostles and disciples was in the realm of discerning of spirits, giving them clear understanding of Satan's attempt to deceive and corrupt the early Church. Peter's reply to Simon the sorcerer, who attempted to buy from John and Peter the ability to impart the Holy Spirit, contained an element of revelation, a discerning of the powers that motivated the man. *'Repent of this wickedness'* challenged Peter, *'and pray to the Lord. Perhaps he will forgive you for having such a thought in your heart. **For I see you are full of bitterness and captive to sin'** (Acts 8:22).

Such incisive revelation by the indwelling Holy Spirit greatly contributed to the forward thrust of the early Church. Now, at the end of the age, as the Church of Jesus surges forward with renewed power and life, that same clear discernment is needed. We need to seek God for the supernatural equipping which is available for us today, and for an increased revelation into the realm of the spirit, in order to carry out effective spiritual warfare.

A strongman revealed

In December 1979, during a visit to Poland, I read an article on 'Binding the Strong Man' by Don Basham. This was based on the words of Jesus we find in Matthew 12:29, and set out how territories and communities were often controlled by evil powers that dominated them from the second heaven. I prayed to the Lord that He would show me how true this was, and to reveal any spiritual 'strong man' that might rule that place. I was sitting in a church meeting as I asked for this revelation, and instantly a very clear picture of a wolf's head came to my mind. It was the Holy Spirit's answer to my request – I believe I had been shown the spiritual power controlling from the heavens.

Later, meditating further upon what I had seen, I understood the wolf to be a revelation of the evil ruling power in the heavens that gave communism its might. Poland at that time was totally under communist control. When the dominating influence of communism was broken in Eastern Europe so suddenly at the end of the 1980s, I believe it was because the ruling power in the heavens was broken by prevailing prayer.

In the books of Daniel and Revelation, dominating world powers are portrayed as wild beasts. There is a lion, a bear, a leopard, and one creature that is a composite of all the others. The symbolic wolf is in keeping with this, and is a very apt symbol for the spiritual power that orchestrated the destructive and oppressive rule of the communist empire in Europe.

As the Holy Spirit continues to lead local churches and individuals into spiritual warfare and ministry to those bound by demons, there will be a growing need to know our enemy and his strategy more clearly.

3

Spiritual Gifts

Corinth be careful

Paul lists the gift of 'discerning of spirits' amongst the nine spiritual gifts he writes of in his first epistle to the Corinthians. From this letter we gather that Paul had received news from the church in Corinth that was causing him some anxiety. The fellowship in Corinth, a good number of them Paul's own converts to Christ, had written asking his advice on a number of issues and Paul's letter contains answers their questions, as well as challenging wrong behaviour in certain areas.

Paul was concerned that the church might become divided by following personalities instead of the Person of Christ. He was concerned about their conduct whenever they met as a church to remember the Lord's death, and also about their understanding of spiritual things.

Paul's desire for this newly established church in Corinth was that the people should be kept strong in their commitment to Christ and free from division. He rejoiced that there was no lack of spiritual gifts in the fellowship, but was keenly aware of the possibility of spiritual deception. It was a very real danger for this church, as the greater part of them came from a background of pagan idol worship with all its demonic connotations. He writes that prior to their conversion they were, *'influenced and led astray to mute idols'* (1 Corinthians 12:2), and that they needed to beware lest they fall under the same influences again. Paul's concern was that they should not be *'ignorant of spiritual gifts'*, but have an understanding of the ways in which the Holy Spirit manifests Himself through individual believers when they come together in the name of Jesus. He longed that they should be prepared and willing for the Holy Spirit to use them in blessing and strengthening each other, whenever they met as the Body of Christ. Paul also warned them to be careful not to confuse the influence and manifestation of the Holy Spirit with that of any evil spirit.

Conflict at the end of the age
This teaching of Paul's is as vital today as it was in those early days of the Church. As we approach the end of the age and the glorious return of Jesus, there is again a great outpouring of the Holy Spirit. There is the 'gathering in' of a mighty harvest into God's kingdom from all parts of the earth as the good news is proclaimed with the demonstration of God's power. At the same time as this advance is being made, there is an upsurge of demonic activity – a renewed satanic opposition to the moving of God's Spirit. Whenever the Holy Spirit has brought revival, the enemy of the Church has sought to counterfeit and bring into disrepute the manifestations of the life of God. He provokes demonic, soulish, and unwise activity amongst God's people to achieve this end, seeking to discredit and marginalise those who want to press forward into the realm of the supernatural in the power of the Holy Spirit. As we experience the supernatural, and are aware of increasing spiritual mani-festations in church gatherings, we need a knowledge of the Scriptures and an understanding of the principles of God's kingdom established in our hearts, together with the direction and discernment of the Holy Spirit.

Spiritual gifts
Paul writes of nine manifestations of the Holy Spirit (spiritual gifts) in order to correct any ignorance the Corinthian believers might have regarding spiritual experiences. He emphasises that it is the 'One Holy Spirit' who chooses to work in a variety of ways, and that there should never be any sense of competition amongst believers when these gifts are in use, nor any contra-diction of the truth as set out in God's Word. *'There are different kinds of gifts, but the same Spirit. There are different kinds of service, but the same Lord. There are different kinds of*

working, but the same God works all of them in all men'
(1 Corinthians 12:4–6).

Three groups of three
The nine gifts may be divided into three groups of three gifts. There are the **vocal gifts**, those spoken out by inspiration of the Holy Spirit, of speaking in tongues, interpretation of tongues, and prophecy; the **power gifts**, demonstrating the power of the Holy Spirit, which are gifts of healing, miracles, and the gift of faith; and the **revelation gifts**, where knowledge is imparted by the Holy Spirit, of word of knowledge, word of wisdom, and discerning of spirits.

What all nine gifts have in common is that they are fully supernatural and do not originate in human reasoning or ability. They are a manifestation, a shining out, of the indwelling Holy Spirit. The revelation gifts – word of knowledge, word of wisdom, and discerning of spirits – are all methods of communication that the Holy Spirit uses reveal certain facts to the believer.

The gift of 'discerning of spirits' is the Holy Spirit's way of revealing to an individual the awareness of the presence, activity or effect, of a spirit being (or beings).

The word translated 'discerning' is the Greek word *diakrisis* which means literally a 'judging through' – and carries the idea of receiving clear information about a thing – a thorough investigation that leaves no doubt.

Nothing is hidden from God's Spirit
The Holy Spirit of God knows all things, and nothing is hidden from His scrutiny or understanding. Scripture presents this truth in a number of ways. John, on the Isle of Patmos, had a revelation of the risen glorified Jesus at the centre of the throne of God in heaven: *'Then I saw a Lamb, looking as if it had been slain ... He had seven horns and seven eyes, which are the seven spirits of God sent out into all the earth'* (Revelation 5:6).

This description echoes that of the Old Testament prophet Zechariah *'These seven are the eyes of the Lord which range throughout the earth'* (Zechariah 4:10). There is no secret place

18

where God does not know what is happening. The use of the number seven in these passages conveys the idea of divine perfection, the seven horns being all-powerful, and the seven eyes all-seeing. King David expressed the truth this way *'Where can I flee from your presence? If I go up to the heavens, you are there; if I make my bed in the depths, you are there. If I rise on the wings of the dawn, if I settle on the far side of the sea, even there your hand will guide me, your right hand will hold me fast. If I say, "Surely the darkness will hide me and the light become night around me," even the darkness will not be dark to you; the night will shine like the day, for darkness is as light to you'* (Psalm 139:7–12).

No activity of any angel or demon is hidden from God and the Holy Spirit is able to share this knowledge with whomever He chooses. The Holy Spirit is responsible for the gifts that any individual member of the Body of Christ might receive: *'He* [the Holy Spirit] *gives them to each one, just as he determines'* (1 Corinthians 12:11). However, we are encouraged to seek the gifts and to *'eagerly desire'* them (1 Corinthians 12:31; 1 Corinthians 14:1).

The gift of discerning of spirits will be given as the Holy Spirit purposes. He will do so when there is a need for the gift, and an openness and eagerness to exercise the gift. As Christians enter into spiritual warfare and begin to take authority over evil spirits in the name of Jesus, the gift will begin to be operated more regularly and with greater understanding.

When a believer has the gift of discerning of spirits it does not mean he will constantly have the secrets of the spirit world unveiled before him. Each act of discernment is a separate revelation. We cannot decide when the gift will operate, that is the prerogative of the Holy Spirit. We can however be prepared and open for the gift to operate.

To see demons all the time is not good
To live constantly aware of every demonic activity and presence would be too much pressure for anyone to take. Life would hardly be bearable. There are some who claim to be in a state of continual demonic awareness. However, the source of their

revelation is probably demonic, rather than the enlightening of the Holy Spirit, and they need setting free from this.

At the time when I was just becoming aware of the reality of deliverance and spiritual warfare, I came under a sustained demonic attack. I had contact with a number of Satanists and spiritists at that time, and there was, what I now consider to be, an attempt by the enemy to hinder a moving forward into the realm of spiritual warfare by me, my wife, and the church where we minister. During this time of acute attack, I was constantly aware of demonic presence and activity, in and around the people I was meeting and seeing. In places I visited I was acutely conscious of the spiritual pressure and control being exercised there. The attack upon myself was eventually broken through prayer and the intense spiritual awareness I had lived with ceased when that victory was won.

I am convinced that it is not God's will for His children to live under such pressure. The gift He has given through the indwelling Holy Spirit is a discernment that comes when needed. I believe that many who are involved in occult activity however, are subject to this demonic pressure and awareness – often seeking to use it for their own ends. I have ministered to Christians who have come from Satanist and spiritist backgrounds who, prior to being set free from occult spirits, claimed that when walking down a street, they knew in which homes they would find those involved in occult or witchcraft practices. It was a supernatural awareness given to them by the occult demons they needed to be set free from. One lady, on receiving deliverance, testified to the sudden and complete ending of such instinctive knowledge which she had lived with from childhood.

4

What Spirits Are There
to Be Discerned?

In the spirit realm we have the activity of God's kingdom and the rebellious activity of Satan's kingdom. Generally when people think of 'discerning of spirits' they think of uncovering the activity of demons, but the gift is able to give insight not only into the intrigues of Satan's kingdom, but also into the ministry of God's angels and the working of the Holy Spirit.

Discerning the Holy Spirit
At times the Holy Spirit can operate in ways that may seem strange to us, in ways other than that which we have previously known or expected. It is important when this happens that we do not judge simply according to our reason or our experience, and that we are open to revelation from the Lord, being sensitive to the prompting and leading of the Holy Spirit. The Pharisees ascribed the works of Christ to Beelzebub – Satan himself – and sadly, religious leaders have at times shown little more understanding than the Pharisees did, often being opposed to revival amongst God's people through lack of spiritual discernment or prejudice.

To dismiss the working of the Holy Spirit as demonic activity is a serious offence against the Lord. We are not however, to blindly accept every supernatural manifestation as from God. The more the power of God is at work, the more we need to be wise in our judgements. God does not want us to be ignorant of spiritual things, and has therefore given us all the help we will need.

The Holy Spirit always acts in agreement with God's Word and according to God's character, and this is initially how we make a judgement about what is taking place. The gift of discerning of spirits has been given so that we should not be left in any doubt as to what is, and is not, of God. When there are supernatural manifestations in the church, and in people's lives, we are not left in uncertainty. The Spirit of God Himself desires to lead us to know the truth, so we should seek Him for discernment, and be open to revelation.

John the Baptist's vision of the Holy Spirit as a dove, descending upon Jesus as He came up from the waters of the Jordan, was a personal revelation – the thousands who thronged the banks of the river saw nothing. This is an example of discerning the presence and activity of the Holy Spirit.

In church meetings there are times when it is possible to 'feel' the presence of the Holy Spirit. Some people describe it as being aware of an 'anointing' on the meeting. This awareness can come to us in a number of ways: with an inner sense of awe, a welling up of emotion, and at other times may seem like a tangible presence.

Some years ago, the leaders of our fellowship spent two days together at Ashburnham Place, where we sought the Lord together, shared our experiences of God's visitation, and prayed for each other. That time together ended with a tremendous sense of the power of God being manifest in the room. We all sat back in our armchairs as if weighted down by the presence of the Lord, no one speaking, just overwhelmed by the power of God. We all left that retreat changed men.

As the Church experiences more of the outpouring of the Holy Spirit, we will need to be increasingly sensitive to God's presence and anointing, and develop the gift of discerning of spirits by waiting on the Lord.

Discerning God's angels
God's angels are constantly at work on His behalf, executing His judgements and fulfilling His purposes. They are active daily on behalf of Christians. The Scriptures tell us they are *'ministering spirits sent to serve those who will inherit salvation'* (Hebrews 1:14), and that *'the angel of the Lord encamps around those who fear him'* (Psalm 34:7). This angelic activity is, for the

most part, unobserved, and we acknowledge the angels' presence because God's Word states that they are there.

The Bible mentions that there are different ranks of angels. In the series of visions the Apostle John received on the Isle of Patmos, the activity of a number of these angels was revealed to him. Each of the seven churches spoken of in the first three chapters of the book of Revelation has an angel who is responsible for them, and is in direct relationship with the risen Christ, the Lord of the Church. John also saw angels releasing God's judgement on the earth – one angel having responsibility over the Abyss, and one with power to restrain the Dragon. Jesus spoke of angels who were responsible for the care of individuals, particularly mentioning children (Matthew 18:10). We read of angels ministering to Jesus in His times of need – in the wilderness after His temptation, and later in the Garden of Gethsemane.

The Bible has numerous accounts of Angels being seen, especially when they come as messengers from the Lord. However, to see an angel is not necessarily the same as having the gift of discerning of spirits. Angels are able to present themselves in a visible form to us, and many angelic visitations are made in this manner. At the birth of Christ, the shepherds on the hillside saw the angels who came with news of Jesus' birth. This would not have been spiritual discernment on the part of the shepherds, but the simply the angels revealing themselves. However, to see angels when they are unseen by others, indicates the gift of discerning of spirits in action, such as when the eyes of Elisha's servant were spiritually opened.

In times of conflict or discouragement, the Holy Spirit is able to give us encouragement and hope by revealing those who contend for us.

Discerning Satan's fallen angels
Satan is the arch-rebel, called in Scripture 'the god of this age'. He is known also as a deceiver, able to disguise himself as an angel of light, so clearly we need the help of the Holy Spirit to stand against his schemes.

He has a host of powers under his control that seek, from the second heaven, to rule over the affairs of men. These are most probably the angels that fell along with Satan when he was cast down from his place of authority in heaven (Isaiah 14:12).

We receive an insight into the structure of Satan's usurped authority in the book of Daniel. Here, the ruling power over the Empire of Persia is called 'the Prince of the Persian Kingdom'. This prince had his position in the second heaven, and was able to resist an angel coming as a messenger from God to Daniel, for a period of twenty-one days, until other angelic help arrived in the form of Michael, one of God's chief Princes (Daniel 10:12–14).

The same passage in Daniel has a prophecy regarding an emerging world power – the Greeks – who conquered the Persians under Alexander the Great. The angel tells Daniel that the 'Prince of Greece' will take the position of the 'Prince of Persia' in the second heaven (Daniel 10:20). What subsequently took place on the earth, was a result of what had already taken place in the heavens.

These powers in the heavens that hold sway over empires, nations, cities and towns, need to be bound and resisted by the people of God. They are some of the 'strong men' that Jesus said it was necessary to 'bind first' before their houses may be plundered. When we do not know much about the strong man, as is often the case, the Holy Spirit can reveal his identity to us and also his function.

Discerning demons
Demons (evil spirits) seek, under the control of their master Satan, to harass, indwell and dominate the bodies of men, women and children. They bring fear, compulsion, sickness, confusion and chaos to those whom God created and loves. Demons hate mankind simply because God loves us. Some who are demonised demonstrate bizarre and clearly demon-motivated behaviour. However, evil spirits will usually seek to operate in secret, and the gift of discerning of spirits is needed to uncover them and their activity wherever their presence is not so obvious.

5

The Ministry of Jesus

The finger of God at work

When Jesus began His preaching and teaching in the towns and villages of Galilee, the crowds attracted to Him were amazed at the healing of the sick, and the authority which He exercised over evil spirits. After a man had been delivered from evil spirits in the synagogue at Capernaum, Mark records the reaction of the people: *'"What is this? A new teaching – and with authority! He even gives orders to evil spirits and they obey him"'* (Mark 1:27). A study of the gospels shows that casting out evil spirits was a major part of the daily work of Jesus. Following this Sabbath day incident we read that, *'That evening after sunset the people brought to Jesus all the sick and demon-possessed. The whole town gathered at the door, and Jesus healed many who had various diseases. He also drove out many demons, but would not let the demons speak because they knew who he was.'* (Mark 1:32–34).

The following day Jesus with His disciples moved on from Capernaum to preach in other surrounding villages, and Mark comments, *'... he travelled throughout Galilee, preaching in their synagogues and driving out demons'* (Mark 1:39).

Herod Antipas, the tetrarch of Galilee, had John the Baptist beheaded because he had publicly denounced his marrying his brother's wife. Hearing of the teaching and growing popularity of another preacher – Jesus, a cousin of the Baptist's – he threatens to take His life as well. Some Pharisees brought this news to Jesus, who in His reply, summed up the work the Father had given Him to do. *'"Go tell that fox I will drive out demons and heal people today and tomorrow, and on the third day I will reach my goal!"'* (Luke 13:32). Jesus evidently considered the release of men, women and children from indwelling evil spirits as a priority in His ministry.

During the three years of His public ministry, Jesus healed and cast demons out of thousands of people. He did it by the power of the Holy Spirit whom He referred to as 'the finger of God': '... if I drive out demons by the finger of God, then the kingdom of God has come to you' (Luke 11:20).

On many occasions the evil spirits in people would be obliged to manifest whenever they came near Him. Such was the anointing upon Jesus that there would be no need for discernment, their presence was clear to all. 'Whenever the evil spirits saw him, they fell down before him and cried out "You are the Son of God"' (Mark 3:11). At other times Jesus would know that there was an evil spirit indwelling those who came before Him by the revelation of the Holy Spirit. He would know when the sick needed deliverance to bring about their healing, as in the case of the blind and dumb man in Matthew 12:22. He would also know the difference between an emotional reaction and a demonic manifestation as He reached out to those in need.

The incident that caused uproar in the synagogue at Capernaum began with a man interrupting Jesus as He was teaching. Jumping up, he began to shout at Jesus '"What do you want with us, Jesus of Nazareth? Have you come to destroy us? I know who you are – the Holy One of God!"' Imagine if, in one of our church services during the preaching, someone in the congregation stood up and yelled at the preacher! This was unusual behaviour for the synagogue! What must others there that day have thought? Jesus had no doubt as to why the man made the sudden outburst, and sternly rebuked the evil spirit. '"Come out of him!" The evil spirit shook the man violently and came out of him with a shriek' (Mark 1:26). Such outbursts of anger, fear, or panic, are often demonic manifestations and we need the discernment that Jesus had to handle such situations with wisdom and authority.

When the charismatic gifts begin to be manifest in congregations of God's people, there comes a fresh liberty for praise and worship. However, this release into greater freedom can often be opposed by 'religious' people, bringing tension and conflict

26

6

Deliverance in the Book of Acts

Luke wrote the book of Acts as the sequel to the gospel named after him. His purpose was to give to Theophilus a clear account of how the Church grew after Jesus ascended to heaven. In his writing he mentions incidents of healing and deliverance that affected the life and growth of the Church. One such incident was the healing of the cripple at the gate of the temple in Acts 3:1–10. This man, leaping about in the temple courts after his amazing healing, drew the attention of the crowds, resulting in the rulers of the Jews forbidding the apostles to preach in the name of Jesus. Luke does not tell us exactly how many people were receiving miracles from God in their lives, but all the time the gospel was being preached, and the believers strengthened and formed into local churches, healing and deliverance was taking place. Luke records Paul's arrival at Corinth, how he worked in the city for eighteen months, but makes no mention of any miracles taking place. However, Paul writing to the Corinthian church, speaks of his preaching amongst them in these terms: *'My message and my preaching were not with wise and persuasive words, but with a demonstration of the Spirit's power...'* (1 Corinthians 2:4), so evidently the miraculous did take place during Paul's stay there.

Although it was not Luke's intention to highlight **all** the miracles and healings that took place during this period of history, he does give us some examples:

Jerusalem
Soon after the healing of the cripple at the Beautiful Gate, the apostles are able to witness with great power. We are told that *'much grace was upon them all'* (Acts 4:33), and *'The apostles*

29

performed many miraculous signs and wonders among the people' (Acts 5:12).

People carried their sick out into the streets, just so the shadow of Peter might fall on them. Acts 5:16 says, *'Crowds gathered also from the towns around Jerusalem, bringing their sick and those tormented by evil spirits, and all of them were healed.'*

Samaria

When persecution broke out against the believers in Jerusalem, following the stoning to death of Stephen, Philip travelled to a city in Samaria and preached Christ there. The miracles that accompanied Philip's preaching caused the inhabitants to take notice, and we read that, *'With shrieks, evil spirits came out of many, and many paralytics and cripples were healed'* (Acts 8:7). I have frequently been in meetings, especially when mention is made of the power the name of Jesus has to cast out demons, where spirits have cried out in much the same way as they did in Philip's meetings in Samaria.

Some years ago I was invited to Montpellier, in the south of France, to preach in a gypsy church. The second evening I was there, I spoke on the danger of being involved in the occult, and how such involvement is an open door for demons to enter into people's lives. I then led the congregation in prayer, asking the Lord's forgiveness and renouncing the occult. There was an immediate reaction throughout the hall as spirits began to manifest and leave people. Some fell to the ground, others began to choke and cough, and a number were set free with loud cries and wailing. Taking part in such times of deliverance brings the passage describing Philip's revival meetings to life. Invariably after such times of release, as in Samaria, there is 'great joy'.

Philippi

In the city of Philippi, Paul confronted and drove out a spirit of divination from a slave girl who had been annoying Paul and Silas for a number of days. When this spirit of divination left the girl she lost her ability to tell fortunes. This is the only case recorded in the Scriptures where a person is set free who seemingly has not put their trust in the Lord, or sought His help to be free (Acts 16:16).

Ephesus

During Paul's time of ministry in Ephesus we read *'God did extraordinary miracles through Paul, so that even handkerchiefs and aprons that had touched him were taken to the sick, and their illnesses were cured and the evil spirits left them'* (Acts 19:11). It would seem from this and other similar verses that the Word God often links sickness with the presence of evil spirits. Of course, not all sickness is linked to demonic activity, but perhaps there is more of a correlation than is generally realised by today's Church.

If God has given us the book of Acts as a pattern for evangelism and the life of the Church until Jesus returns, then we should expect to see similar manifestations of the power of God as the early Church did when we announce the good news of the Kingdom. One of the key factors that has accompanied the revival taking place today in Argentina, has been a keen awareness of the need for spiritual warfare, and a willingness to recognise, confront and cast out demons in believers, and the thousands of new converts to Christ. I believe one of the urgent tasks before the Church is the equipping of believers so that they might be ready to minister effectively into the lives of those who need to be set free.

7

How Does the Gift Operate?

By revelation or by detection?
If someone requests prayer because they believe they might
need deliverance, the presence of spirits can be known by
revelation or by deduction. It is not necessary to have specific
revelation of the demon being present in order to cast it out. If
someone is constantly battling against tormenting fears and
panic attacks, it is not necessary to have revelation. It is obvious
that evil spirits are present.

Very often deliverance is considered as the last resort after
extensive counselling and various disciplines, such as more
Bible study, or prayer and fasting, have not proved successful
in resolving a problem. My experience in this area has taught
me that the need for deliverance is far more necessary than the
majority of Christians realise, and no harm is done by immediately coming against spirits that are probably at work.

A doctor will diagnose an illness by the symptoms his patient
is experiencing, and in much the same way evil spirits can be
detected by their activity in a person's life. As the fruit of the
Holy Spirit is known by love, joy, peace, patience, kindness,
goodness, faithfulness, gentleness and self-control, so evil spirits
are known by their fruit – which includes fear, hatred, anger,
violence, depression etc.

Those who would be used by the Lord to bring freedom to
others, must be willing to pray and confront a possible enemy
presence on the basis of deduction as well as by revelation.

Fear of water
Some years ago I was the guest speaker for a Christian holiday

on the Island of Corfu. Near the hotel, under the cliffs, was a place for the guests to go swimming. The water was fairly deep, and swimmers used a pontoon moored against a small jetty to gain access to the sea. One of the guests, wearing a life jacket, had just climbed out of the water on to the pontoon, and I asked him how he had enjoyed his swim. He shared with me that he had been terrified, and that it was the first time he had ever gone into the sea. He had always had a fear of drowning, and at school he had been excused from swimming classes because it was such a problem for him. I suggested that he might need deliverance from a spirit of fear and we prayed together for a few moments. I commanded a spirit of fear to leave him and he felt tightness in his chest, followed by a release. I then suggested we climb down together into the sea. He followed me apprehensively down the steps, but was soon floating around with the help of his life jacket, free from all anxiety and panic. On my return home I received a letter from him with the news that he was taking swimming lessons at his local pool, and the fears that had troubled him for 40 years were totally gone. When I offered to pray with him, it was not because I had a revelation about a spirit of fear, but the panic he had lived with from a boy was a clear indication of the presence of such a spirit.

On many occasions I have begun to minister deliverance, believing that evil spirits were present, based upon what someone has told me of their condition. It is as I have begun to pray that I have received a revelation as to what specific spirits are present. If we decide only to minister when we have specific revelation, we may deprive many people of the help they need that is provided for them in Christ's victory on the cross.

How the discerning of spirits operates
The Holy Spirit can operate through any of our natural senses to bring awareness of the spirit world, as well as placing a thought into our heart, or giving us a dream or a vision.

The apostle Paul did not want to be like a man who was 'running aimlessly', or fighting as a man 'beating the air'

(1 Corinthians 9:26). He wanted the assurance that his efforts for God's Kingdom were achieving something worthwhile. When as Christians we realise the struggle we have against satanic forces, we do not want to be 'beating the air', but inflicting damage on the powers set against us. We want to 'bind the strong man' in situations of difficulty, so that we can 'enter his house and carry off his treasures' (Matthew 12:29). The Holy Spirit can give us sensitivity to, and knowledge of, the forces of evil in the heavens, so that we may pray effectively against them.

The following examples, mainly from my own experience, will help explain how the Holy Spirit communicates the information to us that He determines we need.

Seeing into the realm of spirits
We have already seen how the servant of Elisha had his 'eyes opened' to see the angels of God who were protecting his master. Our eyes can also be enabled at time to see angels or demons as the Holy Spirits deems necessary.

The monkey
One Sunday evening at the close of a church service, I was praying for a lady who had asked for help. As I prayed with her, she became aware of a strong physical reaction in her legs, which I took to be the manifestation of an evil Spirit. After a few minutes she was set free and rejoined her family who were waiting for her. A young man then approached me to tell me that whilst I was praying for the lady, he had seen what looked like a little monkey running around her legs.

He had received a 'discerning of spirits' and saw the spirit that was being cast out in monkey form. It is worth noting that the revelation revealed the spirit running around outside the person, and yet the evil spirit was actually operating within the person and needed driving out. The discernment clearly showed the demonic activity, but not the precise location of the evil spirit. When we have such a revelation, we must be careful not to attribute more to it than the Holy Spirit is seeking to make known.

A Spanish pastor

Once, I ministered to a pastor in Spain who, as a child, had been taken by his parents to occult healers. He was released from a number of spirits, coughing and choking as he was set free. I literally saw a dark object leave his mouth and fly across the room. It happened very quickly, was not very distinct, and I was left with the thought, 'Did I really see that?' – even though I knew I had indeed seen it. I believe the Holy Spirit enabled me to see that spirit leave the man.

A distorted face

I was once visited at home by a man who, I later discovered, was heavily involved in witchcraft. We were talking about the claims of the gospel to which he was violently opposed. As I looked at him his face seemed to become very ugly and I surprised my wife and myself by saying to him 'You are very ugly!' I've never said such a thing to anyone before or since. After he left our house my wife wanted to know why I had been so rude to him. She thought he was rather handsome and not ugly at all.

All I could say was that at that moment when I spoke out, I had been shocked by the ugliness that had appeared. This man had begun a friendship with one of the young ladies attending our church. I never saw him again, and thankfully, the relationship with the girl was soon broken off. The Holy Spirit caused me to see in his features something of the demons that operated in him.

The sufferings of Mary

I have at times prayed for people for deliverance, and seen in the expression that came over their face, a glimpse of the spirit they needed to be set free from.

During a seminar I was helping to conduct in France, my wife and I were approached by a young woman who asked if we would pray for her to be free from certain ongoing pressures in her life. As we prayed and began to address any demonic beings oppressing her, she went into a trance like state with a very strange expression on her face. Her head lifted to one side, her eyes gazed up, and there was an intense look of agony and sorrow. As I watched her, I thought I had seen that expression before. Then I recalled that in certain Catholic churches there is often a sculpture, supposedly representing the mother of Jesus holding His crucified, dead body in her arms. The expression on Mary's face in this sculpture was exactly what I saw on the French girl's face.

I rebuked any spirit associated with the idea of 'the sufferings of Mary' and immediately there was a reaction from the girl. With a scream she was set free from the spirit manifesting in her. Later she explained that as a child she had been dedicated to the Virgin Mary. I believe such a dedication to a dead person can open the door to an evil spirit.

Discernment in dreams

God will, at times, speak to us through dreams. The Bible records various instances in which He has chosen to make His purposes known using this method. Joseph had a dream that foretold a time when his father and brothers would bow down to him (Genesis 37:5). Jacob dreamt of a stairway reaching up to heaven (Genesis 28:12). The wise men from the East, who came to find the baby Jesus, were warned in a dream not to return to see King Herod, but to return home via another route (Matthew 2:12). The ungodly also received dreams from God, warning them of His displeasure and threatening judgement – notable examples being the Pharaoh of Egypt at the time of Moses, and Nebuchadnezzar, the Babylonian despot.

God said that He would make Himself known to His prophets by visions and dreams. Numbers 12:6 says, *'When a prophet of the Lord is among you, I reveal myself to him in visions, I speak to him in dreams.'* This is also emphasised by the prophet Joel, whom Peter quoted on the day of Pentecost:

'In the last days, God says, I will pour out my Spirit on all people. Your sons and daughters will prophesy, your young men will see visions, your old men will dream dreams.'

(Acts 2:17).

36

Roman remains

In 1981, my wife and I travelled by car to the south of France, for a series of meetings we were to take at the Assemblies of God Church in Hyeres. We stopped for the night at the town of Orange, staying in a small hotel near the town centre. That night I found it very difficult to sleep and sensed an atmosphere of aggression. There were angry voices in the street, and when I did eventually doze off, I dreamt of violence and confrontation.

The next morning we visited the town and saw the remains of a Roman amphitheatre, built in the time of Augustus, and a Roman triumphal arch erected to commemorate the victories of Julius Caesar. The site of the town had been the scene of much violence in the past, and the area had originally been settled by ex-legionaries who had been given tracts of land when they left the Roman legions. The spiritual powers ruling the area brought a sense aggression to the town. No doubt the events of the past – the violence and bloodshed – were linked with the spiritual domination of the area.

My disturbed night was due to the sensitivity the Holy Spirit was giving me to discern the influence of the 'strong man' dominating the region.

Death like a black cloud

The International Bible Training Institute (IBTI) at Burgess Hill in Sussex has a 'Camp Convention' each year in the month of August. Staff and students are joined by Christians from various churches with their tents and caravans, and meetings are conducted all week in a large tent set in the grounds of the Bible School.

At one such camp in 1982, our family had set up our tent with the other campers and was enjoying the Convention week. One of the resident lecturers of the IBTI, Jean-Jacques Zbinden, was very ill at the time. He had undergone open-heart surgery and had various complications following the operation. He was not expected to live very long.

Early one morning I had a vivid dream. I was in a lecture room together with a number of people who were standing around Jean-Jacques, praying for him. In the dream I moved to the back of the room and looked across the praying group. As I did, I saw a black cloud enveloping the sick man. It was isolating him from those praying. I pointed to the cloud and rebuked it in the name of Jesus. I then awoke with this picture and the details very clear in my mind.

I recounted the dream to a number of friends who were sharing in the camp ministry that week, and to my brother Philip. Later that day, we went to the room where the dying man was in bed. I told him about the dream, and then took authority over the spirits which were responsible for the sickness. After prayer, John-Jacques said that although he felt different physically, something had happened in his spirit – he felt a lightening, a release. A short time later he was fully restored physically and resumed his duties in the Bible School.

Many people had been praying for his healing, but it was necessary to confront the evil spirits at work and drive them out – as the dream I received had indicated. The Holy Spirit was revealing the reason why the sickness had such a tenacious hold. Today, 18 years later, Jean-Jacques is still in good health and continues his work at the IBTI.

8

Operation of the Gift Continued

Discernment by hearing
The Holy Spirit is able to quicken any of our natural senses in order to bring revelation. We have considered examples of how our eyes can at times see that which is normally not visible. The same can happen with our hearing – our ears being opened to receive revelation.

Hearing the wind
A visiting evangelist, Henry Shave, spoke one Friday evening at our church in Croydon. During the time of worship and prayer at the beginning of the meeting, I heard a roaring noise that I thought at first was an aeroplane. After a short while I realised the sound was in fact inside the building, and seemed to move down the left side of the hall from the front to the back. As far as I could discover afterwards, only one other person present that evening heard 'the wind' blowing through the church.

Back at home later that evening, I told Henry about my experience, and he shared with me how that in the afternoon before coming up to Croydon, the Lord had spoken to him from the book of Ezekiel where the prophet is told *'prophesy to the wind son of man'* (Ezekiel 37:9). He had then prayed what he felt the Holy Spirit was prompting him to pray – that the wind of God, the Holy Spirit, would be manifest in the meetings at Croydon, and that 'the wind would blow'.

There had indeed been a particular anointing of the Holy Spirit that night for people to be healed and baptised in the Holy Spirit. I felt privileged to hear, in such a remarkable way, what God had been preparing to do that night.

It blows again

The next day, Henry and I visited the apartment of a couple in the fellowship who had been under spiritual pressure for some time. The people living in the apartment above them were spiritists, and Don and Sue felt their home was being affected by their occult activity. As we prayed in the home, I again heard the noise like a wind blowing. This time it was more violent and seemed to come from the rooms above. It gave me the impression of a whirlwind sweeping through and cleansing the place. As we were entering into spiritual warfare against any demonic activity or presence on the floor above, the Holy Spirit began a work of cleansing – driving out the enemy and bringing in God's peace. Again I was privileged to hear it taking place.

Spiritual eavesdropping

On one occasion, myself and one of our ministry team were asked to pray for a young woman at the close of one of our services. She was someone who often asked for counsel and prayer. Before beginning, I distinctly heard two voices talking together. The conversation went like this: 'They will never get us out ... we'll keep them here for hours.' In this instance we felt it right not to pray for the young lady, having carefully considered that which we felt to be God's leading for the situation. The Holy Spirit had made clear to us the demons' intention to waste our time. The young woman continued to attend the fellowship, and gradually with teaching and encouragement, became less of an attention seeker. In time she received prayer for deliverance.

Sometimes, we will be confronted with a person that it would be wiser not to minister deliverance to at that time. We can always trust the Holy Spirit to give us His leading in such cases.

The broken spell

A lady, who had been involved in witchcraft for many years, began to attend our fellowship. She had been drawn into a circle of occult practice as a young dancer, after being drugged and abused by someone she called her 'Master'. This man then sought to dominate her life with considerable success for many years.

She had made attempts to break free from this control – this was one of the reasons for seeking out our church – but at certain times in the year, particularly at full moon, she would act as if mesmerised.

One Saturday afternoon I visited her home with Paul, our foster son. We found her in a trance-like state, and she was rather flustered to see us. We were invited to sit down in her lounge whilst she finished some task in another room. To my surprise, I heard a voice that seemed to come from the speakers of a record player. The voice said 'It's no good, our power is broken now.' When I checked the record player, it was definitely turned off. Our presence in her flat that afternoon, as ones who loved and served Jesus, was enough to frustrate the witchcraft being practised on that dear lady.

Truly, '... *the one who is in you is greater than the one who is in the world*' (1 John 4:4). The Holy Spirit enabled me to hear the consternation of the enemy. That lady is still attending our church and has made great progress in the Lord, no longer under that heavy control.

A lion on the prowl
During the early days of my involvement in deliverance, all my family came under strong spiritual attack. Satan sought to intimidate us and to discredit our testimony, so as to make us ineffectual in spiritual warfare, and to prevent us realising the promises God had given regarding exercising authority over demonic power. The fact that a number of people with strong occult backgrounds became involved in our lives at that time, was no coincidence and contributed to the enemy's onslaught.

As we were evidently under some pressure, the church elders suggested that we should take a family holiday. January not being the warmest of months for a vacation in England, we decided to take up a friends invitation and visit him at his home in Majorca. It took a few days to arrange the airline tickets, so up to the day of our flight we stayed with Chris and Elaine, friends from the church.

Our son Nathanael, then 22 months old, was sleeping in a carrycot at the foot of our bed. I was lying awake in the early hours of the morning, when I heard a noise. It sounded like a large animal padding across the floor to where Nathanael was asleep. As I heard it I knew immediately, by revelation, that it was a demonic attack on our son – a spirit coming like a lion, seeking to destroy him.

I immediately woke Doris, who picked up the baby. As she held him, I sought to place my hand on his head and pray for him. Nathanael began to cry and wail – at the same time pushing my hand away. As we persisted in prayer, rebuking the enemy in the name of Jesus, Nathanael began to cough and some greenish phlegm seemed to pump out of his stomach. He finally went limp as if unconscious, and my wife thought he was dying. At that moment, however, I had a complete and total assurance that he was going to be all right. I believe that absolute conviction that he would be well, was given to me as a gift of faith. The Holy Spirit had made known to me that a demon was attacking my son by supernaturally opening my ears, and then assured me of his safety.

Nathanael did not recover immediately. On the flight to Majorca, and for a number of days afterwards, he looked very ill and lost considerable weight. But, during all that time, the conviction that he would be fully restored never left me – even during two other strange incidents that happened on the island.

A spot of light and a carved lion head
The family eventually arrived at our destination in Majorca, travel-weary and somewhat spiritually 'shell-shocked'. We managed to get all the children to bed that night, baby Nathanael sleeping in the room next to ours. As I lay awake early the next morning, I heard Nathanael get out of his bed and toddle out into the corridor. I slipped out of bed and went to fetch him into our bedroom. When I found him, he was walking along the tiled landing towards a marbled staircase leading to the ground floor. He was watching something very intently and following it. Then I noticed a spot of light that was moving along in front of him, and I knew this was an attempt

42

by the enemy to kill or injure the child. The light was leading him to the top of the stairs where it would no doubt have caused him to fall. I reached out to put my hand on the spot of light and it was gone. At the same moment, Nathanael dropped off to sleep and I had to carry him to our bed. I had once again been alerted through the discerning of spirits to the attack on our boy and was able to frustrate it.

Nathanael remained asleep, or possibly in a coma, all that morning. Doris held him all through breakfast, and during a short walk to the beach and back to the house again. On entering the house, Doris intended to put him into his bed, and began to carry him up the stairs. At the bottom of the stairs there was a large, carved wooden post, that supported the banister rail. The ornate carving on this post was a lion's head, and as his mother carried the unconscious child past it, he opened his eyes, smiled at the post, and then dropped back to sleep.

That afternoon we booked in to a nearby hotel, and in our room I began a time of intense spiritual warfare, speaking out against whatever was attacking us in the Name of Jesus, and making mention of our trust in His precious shed blood. I'm not sure how long I continued this battle, perhaps for an hour, but after some time, I suddenly I had the impression in my spirit that something had been broken. The battle was won that evening in the hotel room, and we were able to take three weeks rest in Majorca. Nathanael recovered his strength and appetite, and is today very involved in serving the Lord – preaching and teaching – especially among young people.

Discernment by feeling and the sense of touch
Job said '*A spirit glided past my face, and the hair on my body stood on end*' (Job 4:15). Our sense of touch, and also that which we feel, can be made sensitive by the Holy Spirit, to bring us to an awareness of what is taking place spiritually. Perhaps it is possible that before the fall, Adam's senses were greatly heightened – at all times acutely aware of the spiritual world around him? The cutting off from God, and the curse that came as a result of his disobedience, has affected mankind ever since. As the indwelling Holy Spirit gives us revelation of the spiritual

world, it may be a restoration in part of that which Adam lost. When Jesus returns, and we are changed to be like Him, '... *when the perishable has been clothed with the imperishable...*' (1 Corinthians 15:54), then those abilities will be fully restored.

When there is a particular anointing of the Holy Spirit in a meeting, it is sometimes possible to actually 'feel' the heightened activity of the Spirit of God. Many Christians have this experience, and it is another example of the gift of discerning of spirits in operation.

Often the presence of the Holy Spirit conveys a sense of well being and peace. Conversely, a demonic presence will often bring unease and disquiet.

Under the stairs

I was asked to visit the home of Eva, a lady who had recently come to a knowledge of Jesus as her Saviour and Lord. She wanted me to pray through the house that God's peace might rule there (Luke 10:5). She especially wanted me to pray in her son's bedroom. The son at that time, had no interest in the gospel at all.

I prayed with her in the downstairs rooms, and as we climbed the stairs to pray on the first floor I felt a strange coldness. I mentioned this to Eva and we prayed on the stairs before continuing to visit the other rooms in the house.

Some weeks later, she spoke with me at the close of a Sunday morning meeting, and was quite excited over something she had found in the cupboard under the stairs. Her daughter, who had left home, had stored some of her belongings in the cupboard, and amongst them Eva found a number of books on the occult and a pack of tarot cards, used for fortune-telling. These items were immediately consigned to the rubbish bin. To keep such books and objects in our homes is an invitation for demons to enter. The strange coldness I had felt was a notification by the Spirit that there was something amiss.

A Polish water diviner loses his power

There is evidently a satanic counterfeit of the gift of discerning

44

of spirits. An evil spirit – a spirit of divination – may communicate knowledge of the spirit world. Fortune-tellers and those who use divination to gain knowledge of people's lives, will often ask for an item of jewellery or clothing from the person who consults them, and as they hold it will say they are receiving revelation. They will, at times, claim to sense the presence of 'spirit beings' and refer to how warm or cold they feel in certain places. Any revelation they may receive, however, is demonic in origin and no Christian should ever seek help from such a person, or put any confidence in what such people say.

Deuteronomy 18:10–12 says, *'Let no-one be found among you ... who practices divination or sorcery, interprets omens, engages in witchcraft, or casts spells, or who is a medium or spiritist or who consults the dead. Anyone who does these things is detestable to the Lord...'*

The following incident shows how the counterfeit operates.

At the close of an evangelistic meeting in the south of Poland, I was approached by a man in his 40s who had raised his hand during the service as an indication of his desire to accept Christ. Holding his hands out towards me with the palms a little apart he asked me to place my hand between his. With the help of my interpreter, I asked him why he wanted me to do this. His reply was, 'Please do it.' I held up my hand between his, and he said, 'Ah, that's power.' When I asked why he said that, he replied it was his 'gift from God', and revealed that he worked as a diviner dousing for water sources on the farms. I told him that his 'gift' was not from God, but an occult power, but he was adamant that it was good and God's gift.

I asked him if he would still want this gift it if were truly not of God, and he confirmed that he would not, so I laid my hand on his head and commanded the spirit of divination to leave him in the name of Jesus. He gave a sudden gasp then, looking at his hands, exclaimed, 'Oh, it's gone.'

As the evil spirit left him, the vibrations he used to feel in his hands, that had previously guided him, stopped immediately – just as the slave girl in Philippi lost her ability to tell fortunes when Paul prayed for her deliverance. Water divining is an occult activity, and the sensations felt when a water source is located are demonic in origin.

The wind blows another time
Muriel Shelbourne visited our fellowship to speak at the Bible School, and during her stay testified to a meeting of our Home Group leaders about a move of the Holy Spirit and a time of refreshing that was being experienced in her home church in Lincoln. After sharing what God was doing, Muriel was invited to pray for those present. That evening there was a powerful move of God and the sixty leaders present were greatly blessed. Some, as the Holy Spirit moved, fell to the floor under an anointing, others began to weep, some to laugh and rejoice in the Lord. Quite a number testified later that as Muriel stretched out her hands to pray for them they felt a wind blowing in their faces. They discerned the moving of the Holy Spirit coming upon them through the sense of touch.

Books for burning
A Reformed Pastor in the Swiss town of Neufchatel was given a collection of books by one of his elderly lady parishioners. They were all on the subject of spiritism, the paranormal, and faith healing. I spoke at his church on the dangers of occult involvement, and during a time of fellowship together after the meeting, he showed us the box of books and suggested we take them away and dispose of them.

We returned to a friend's farm where we were staying with the books in the boot of the car. It was not until the following afternoon that we remembered them, and brought the box into the farm kitchen. The four of us who were there began to experience pains in the head as we examined the books. Taking the box of books out to the boiler room, we burnt them all, and at once the headaches ceased.

As we are open to the Lord's leading and willing to wait on Him, I am sure that our sensitivity to spiritual influence will become keener and we will be more discerning and aware of the spiritual world around us.

A childhood injury

A South African lady asked if I would meet with her and her husband in the hope that I might be able to pray with him and help him. Her husband was a man subject to many fears and was unable to make friends. She felt sure that he needed deliverance. They came to my home one evening, although he was there only to please his wife, not at all convinced that he needed ministry. He agreed however, that we could pray together and ask for the Lord's guidance. As we prayed, I felt a pain in my left eye which I took to be a prompting of the Holy Spirit. I asked John if he had ever been injured in the eye. Surprised, he said that as a boy he had nearly lost one of his eyes when another lad had poked him in the face with a stick. I said, 'Was it the left eye?' and immediately his reservations were gone, and he was eager to be prayed for.

He was set free from spirits of fear, and also a spirit that had entered during the time of trauma when he had experienced the injury to his eye. The discernment prepared a fearful brother to receive the help he so needed.

Nausea

On a number of occasions I have been made aware of demonic activity by a feeling of nausea that has swept over me.

A couple who had recently returned to England from Zimbabwe asked me to pray in their home, as they felt oppressed there. Sitting down with them in their living room, we talked for a while and then began to seek the Lord's help, asking Him to reveal the reason for the sense of heaviness they were experiencing. As we turned to prayer, an evil queasiness swept over me. Glancing around the room my attention was drawn to a carved wooden African figure on a shelf, and I felt that this was the cause of the problem. I have learned to accept such impressions as the probable leading of the Holy Spirit.

The husband took down the figure and put it in the rubbish bin by their side gate. Immediately the sensation of nausea stopped. We prayed in the room together, and later the couple confirmed that the sense of heaviness in their home had gone.

We need to be aware that certain objects can attract demons, and be careful not to bring them into our homes. To keep them is to give the enemy an entrance into our lives.

I personally would not want objects or pictures in my home that portrayed heathen gods, any idols, representations of witches or evil spirits, items that had been used in any occult practice, or figures that have an occult connection such as snakes, owls, spiders etc.

Israel was commanded by God not to take into their homes any of the objects belonging to the corrupt nations who were driven out of the Promised Land (Deuteronomy 7:25–26).

Many Christians seem unaware of these dangers and often decorate their homes with objects associated with false religion and idol worship.

There are times when we may receive a revelation from God concerning items that are a snare, but we are also to use our own wisdom and discretion as to what may be foolish for us to keep. There are also certain books it would be better for Christians not to keep on their shelves. When the church in Ephesus experienced a revival, they had a bonfire of books used in 'curious arts – books that were valued at fifty thousand pieces of silver (Acts 19:19).

That feeling again

Some years ago, as I drove into a town in the north-east of France, I once again felt nausea coming over me, and was reminded me of the incident with the African figure. It stayed with me until I had driven through and out of the town. I believe that there was a ruling spirit with a strong hold over that town, and the Holy Spirit was bringing the fact to my attention.

On another occasion, I attended a ministers conference in England, arranged to discuss some difficult issues in the Church that were a cause for concern at the time. On the way there, and during the opening session, I remember having the same unease and queasiness. The conference was a very difficult one with some bitter exchanges and little progress towards resolving the issues being discussed. I believe that there was demonic interference in that meeting, provoking the unpleasantness and harsh attitudes that were being voiced.

On reflection, if I had taken more notice of the warning sign given to me that there was something spiritually wrong, then the spirit responsible for the dissension that day could have been bound in the name of Jesus. The conference would have proceeded more sweetly and much more progress would have been made.

A camp meeting transformed

I experienced a similar discernment when positive action brought about a remarkable change at a Family Bible Camp held at Peterborough in the English East Midlands.

I attended an evening celebration meeting in a large tent set up on the local Show Ground. Sitting amongst the congregation of several hundred, I felt that same nausea. A friend – Rob Ferguson – and myself were at the back of the tent next to the mixing console controlling the microphones and lighting. I told him that I sensed the meeting was under some spiritual attack, and he said that he would agree with me in prayer to bind up whatever was causing the opposition.

We began to speak out against the powers of darkness quietly from our seats, not disturbing the meeting in any way. Up to that moment the meeting had been rather heavy, without much life or any sense of God's anointing.

The brother leading the worship, who normally was full of life, was obviously finding things difficult. As Rob and I prayed, I turned, and pointing my finger towards the platform said, 'The spirit that restricts my brother, I bind you in the name of Jesus.' Just as I said those words, the worship leader began to sing a prophetic word and the whole atmosphere in the tent changed. That night healings took place and the congregation sensed a powerful anointing of the Holy Spirit.

Gatherings of God's people are obviously targets for satanic opposition and we need the gift of discerning of spirits to enable us to resist and counter his strategies effectively.

It is possible that Christians are prompted by the Holy Spirit, receiving discernment, and yet are not aware that it is the

Lord's leading. The occasions that I have recounted, when I was alerted by the feelings of nausea, could easily have been dismissed as nothing more than an upset stomach. It would be wrong however, to suggest that an attack of indigestion or some other physical ailment must always have some spiritual significance. We need to be open to the leading and teaching of the Holy Spirit, and grow in awareness and sensitivity to His prompting and leading.

9

Discernment by a Word of Knowledge

A 'word of knowledge' comes when the Holy Spirit brings a thought or understanding to our mind by revelation. We are aware of a truth, something that has happened or is happening, and that awareness is not by our observation or deduction but by inspiration.

Most instances of discerning of spirits that I have received when seeking to minister to people have come in this way, and usually as I am praying with the person. It is not uncommon for their response afterwards to be 'How did you know those things' or 'you were spot on when you dealt with that.'

I am able then to make the point that if the Holy Spirit is revealing those things it is because the Lord wants the person to be set free, and that they should be encouraged with such tokens of God's favour towards them.

The truth brings freedom

I visited a lady who had requested prayer, accompanied by another sister from our fellowship. If possible, it is a wise practice to have someone else with you if you are going to pray for deliverance. We talked with this sister about the various problems and pressures she was experiencing, and then began to pray. Nothing seemed to be happening however, and we got the sense that there was a spiritual impasse. I sought the Lord to know why this was and the word 'incest' came into my mind. It would have been very easy to dismiss the thought, but I have learned to act even on such gentle prompting. It was not easy to suggest that such a thing may have taken place in her life, so I asked if there was a possibility of any history of incest in her family. She began to cry and told us that she had been involved.

As a teenager she had been molested by an older brother, but had kept it a secret ever since, ashamed of what had taken place. She would never have spoken of it to us, but the Holy Spirit had shown the way that certain spirits had entered her life. She forgave her brother and when we commanded the evil spirits that had entered at that time of trauma to go, she was set free.

Those who minister deliverance need to be compassionate people, and their motive for becoming involved is love for men and women in distress. Care must always be taken to spare those who come for help, any unnecessary anguish and hurt.

Revelations

Christian counsellors need to be very careful regarding revelations they believe they have received of someone's past experiences. It is not always necessary to divulge a word of knowledge, and to do so can in some circumstances bring unnecessary distress. If, for example, a man and wife were being prayed with together and an unpleasant incident from one of their pasts was made known, it could cause hurt to the partner and put a strain on their relationship.

Sadly, some have been told that they have been abused in the past, or that tragic, evil or vile things have been done to them which they have apparently forgotten, when in fact these things never happened. Such suggestions can cause great confusion in a person's life creating suspicion and fear. I am very cautious about supposed witchcraft or Satanist activities that are alleged to have taken place in the family many generations ago. I am of the opinion that such 'revelations' are often little more than the over-active imaginations of well-meaning helpers. Those who give out 'words of knowledge' need to be sure of the source and truth of such revelation.

Not ritual abuse just rejection

A brother was referred to me for help by one of our church counsellors because he was rather disturbed by the man's story. The man attended one of the Saturday mornings that we set aside to help those who are in need of deliverance and claimed that he needed to be set free from the results of satanic abuse that had taken place when he was a young child. On speaking with him I learned that he had no memory of any such abuse having taken place, and there was no indication that his family had any involvement at all with occult or Satanist activity. His conviction that abuse had occurred was a result of someone in the past telling him they had received a picture in their mind of him, as a young child, in a satanic ritual.

The man did need deliverance help, and when ministered to manifested in a very noisy and angry manner, but the problem was not due to any ritual abuse, but spirits that had come in with rejection and relationship problems with his father.

Some associate any demonic problem with occult practice, but this is not so. Occult involvement is but one of the many ways demons can enter the lives of men, women and children.

Impertinence
During a visit to Poland a young man who said he needed deliverance approached me. When I asked him what he needed delivering from, he would not tell me, insisting that the Holy Spirit would have to show me. I declined to pray for him, telling him it was impertinent on his part to expect the Holy Spirit to reveal to me what he could readily share. It is the prerogative of the Holy Spirit to provide us with help as He sees fit. Naturally, such discernment may be sought, but it should not be demanded by us. Those who demand supernatural revelation are in danger of receiving it from a wrong source, and can fall into deception, giving heed to spirits of divination.

The need for discernment during times of spiritual refreshing
Many churches and fellowships have recently been experiencing outpourings of the Holy Spirit, accompanied by various, and at times surprising, manifestations. Some have caused quite a stir and have been reported on TV and in national newspapers. People attending meetings have been reacting in unusual ways – falling down, laughing, crying, shaking, and making strange noises – at times, it seems, quite involuntarily.

When the Holy Spirit moves powerfully on a company of people, there is bound to be a reaction. Some experience great peace, others joy, and there will be those who are experiencing a release in their emotions. The crowd who gathered to see the disciples on the day of Pentecost thought they were drunk – their behaviour, after they were baptised in the Holy Spirit, seemed so bizarre to the onlookers.

When the Holy Spirit is at work in such a way, it is quite common for demons to be agitated and to manifest. Where there is a failure to understand that certain manifestations can be demonic, all manifestations may be attributed to the Holy Spirit's activity and considered as good. Some have sought to identify certain manifestations as being possible prophetic signs of God imparting spiritual gifts, or empowering His people for a particular work.

I heard a young man in one such meeting being encouraged to believe that the manifestation of pins and needles he was feeling about the mouth and jaw, indicated the imparting of a prophetic gift. However in my experience, such a manifestation could indicate the presence of an evil spirit linked to past occult involvement by the family, and when such spirits are challenged and cast out, the manifestation stops immediately.

A gift for our day

As we experience more of the moving of the Holy Spirit in our churches and in the gatherings of God's people, we will need greater wisdom and a fuller understanding of the moving of God's Spirit.

Thankfully we are not left to our own, surmising and fallible judgement, but the gift of discerning of spirits will help us distinguish between the demonic, the emotional reaction, and the Holy Spirit. We need to seek for the gift of discerning of spirits and look for its development in our lives. Paul writing to the church at Corinth, who were experiencing many supernatural manifestations, was keen that they should *'not be ignorant'* about spiritual gifts (1 Corinthians 12:1), and that they should be able to tell when someone was 'speaking by the

Spirit' – meaning the Holy Spirit – or if the inspiration was from a wrong spirit (verses 2–3).

The task is ours

As in the days of the Old Testament, when God spoke at different times and in different ways (Hebrews 1:1), so today the Holy Spirit can use various ways to bring us the revelation we need to do the 'works of the kingdom'.

I trust that the examples I have given have been an encouragement and a help to you. Maybe you have discovered that the Lord is already moving you forward in this gift.

The commission given by Jesus to His disciples is still the same: 'Preach the gospel, heal the sick and cast out demons.' It is the task that is presented to us for our generation.

I realise that those who hold that a Christian cannot need deliverance from evil spirits will be sceptical regarding the experiences I have described in this book, and may believe them to be false or imagined. I was once of that opinion myself, because it is what I was taught as a young man. However, my experiences over the past twenty years, and personal study of the Scriptures have convinced me otherwise. I would ask that those who have such doubts simply to seek God for His direction and wisdom.

To those already engaged in the battle I encourage you to 'fight the good fight' and keep full of the Holy Ghost.

Other titles available in the *What Christians Should Know About...* series:

Depression, Anxiety, Mood Swings and Hyperactivity Dr Grant Mullen

The Endtime Harvest David Shibley

Escaping from Debt Keith Tondeur

Generational Sin Pennant Jones

The Glory of God Ed Roebert

How to Pray Effectively for Your Lost Loved Ones David Alsobrook

The Importance of Forgiveness John Arnott

A Personal Relationship with God Peter Nodding

Preparing for Christ's Return Clive Corfield

Reconciliation John Dawson

Sickness and Healing Ed Harding

Their Value to God Steve and Chris Hepden

Power Filled Worship Russ Hughes

Religious Spirits Rick Joyner

If you have enjoyed this book and would like
to help us to send a copy of it and many other titles
to needy pastors in the **Third World**,
please write for further information
or send your gift to:

**Sovereign World Trust
PO Box 777, Tonbridge
Kent TN11 0ZS
United Kingdom**

or to the **'Sovereign World'** distributor in your country.

Visit our website at **www.sovereign-world.org**
for a full range of Sovereign World books.
